FAR-OUT and UNUSUAL

UNUSUAL

pets

Boas and Pythons

Cool Pets!

Enslow Elementary
an imprint of
Enslow Publishers, Inc.
40 Industrial Road
Box 398
Berkeley Heights, NJ 07922
USA

http://www.enslow.com

Alvin and Virginia
Silverstein and Laura
Silverstein Nunn

Enslow Elementary, an imprint of Enslow Publishers, Inc.

Enslow Elementary® is a registered trademark of Enslow Publishers, Inc.

Library of Congress Cataloging-in-Publication Data

Silverstein, Alvin.
  Boas and pythons : cool pets! / by Alvin Silverstein, Virginia Silverstein and Laura Silverstein Nunn.
    p. cm.
  Includes index.
  Summary: "Provides basic information about boas and pythons and keeping them as pets"—
Provided by publisher.
  ISBN 978-0-7660-3878-3
  1. Boa constrictors as pets—Juvenile literature. 2. Pythons as pets—Juvenile literature. I.
Silverstein, Virginia B. II. Nunn, Laura Silverstein. III. Title.
  SF459.S5S55 2011
  639.3'967—dc22

                                      2011003335

Future editions:
Paperback ISBN 978-1-4644-0129-9

ePUB ISBN 978-1-4645-1036-6

PDF ISBN 978-1-4646-1036-3

Printed in the United States of America

012012 The HF Group, North Manchester, IN

10 9 8 7 6 5 4 3 2 1

To Our Readers: We have done our best to make sure all Internet Addresses in this book were
active and appropriate when we went to press. However, the author and the publisher have no
control over and assume no liability for the material available on those Internet sites or on other Web
sites they may link to. Any comments or suggestions can be sent by e-mail to comments@enslow.com
or to the address on the back cover.

Photo Credits: © 1999 Artville, LLC, p. 12; Alamy: ©81a, p. 43, © John Cancalosi, p. 14
(bottom), © Paul Wood, p. 41, © Stuart Corlett, 13; AP Images: Lynne Sladky, p. 32, Stephen
Nowers, p. 37, Tiffany Tompkins-Condie, p. 30; AP Images/Journal Inquirer, Jim Michaud, p. 8;
© Barbara Stitzer/PhotoEdit, p. 7; © iStockphoto.com: Alfredo Maiquez, p. 16, Paul Tessier,
p. 14 (top), VMJones, p. 4; Jim Crossley, p. 40 (inset); © McDonald Wildlife Photography/Animals
Animals, p. 9; Scott Ableman, p. 40; Shutterstock.com, pp. 1, 3, 10, 11, 15, 19, 21, 22, 23, 25,
26, 29, 34, 38.

Illustration Credits: © 2011 Gerald Kelley, www.geraldkelley.com

Cover Photo: Shutterstock.com

Contents

Even though some people think snakes are dangerous, certain kinds are safe to have as pets, as long as the owner is careful! This snake is a python.

1

Snuggly Snakes

Do you jump at the sight of a little snake in the grass? Lots of people are afraid of snakes. Maybe that's because of the sneaky way a snake slithers through the grass. Or the way its tongue quickly darts in and out like it's about to sting you. But not all snakes are as dangerous as they look. In fact, most snakes are actually harmless.

If you think a little snake looks creepy, imagine a 10-foot (3-meter) snake in your living room! Boa constrictors and pythons are famous for their enormous size. They look like they could

5

Far Out!

Twist and Turn

Ever watch a snake slither along the ground? It twists and turns its body. It bends very easily. The snake looks as if it doesn't have a bone in its body. Actually, snakes do have bones—lots of them!

A large python can have 400 bones or more in its backbone. All these bones let the snake twist and turn easily in many directions. The average man has only 33 bones in his backbone. That is why a snake can coil (twist) its body around and we cannot.

A big snake can make a great pet, but it is also a big responsibility!

easily have you for lunch. But many people actually keep these big snakes for pets. They say that these big guys are not man-eaters, like some people think. Some are actually very calm and friendly.

But don't rush out and get yourself a big snake. Boas and pythons should not be a first choice as a beginner pet. No matter how friendly big snakes may seem, they can be dangerous. Snakes have been known to escape from their cages, and sometimes cause harm.

Boas and pythons are famous for their "hugs." But it's not a friendly snuggle. A big squeeze from one of these snakes can be deadly. That's how

Far Out!

Is It Legal To Have a Boa or Python?

Before you buy a boa or python, make sure you are allowed to own one in your town. Many towns have laws against owning a constrictor, and police may take it away. Some places let you keep them if you have a special permit.

boas and pythons kill their food. They wrap their bodies around an animal and squeeze tight. They keep squeezing until the animal is dead.

People should learn everything they can about boas and pythons before they decide to get one. As long as they are cared for properly, these snakes can be safe to own. They can even be tamed and handled. They are not for everyone, though. Boas and pythons are not for families with small children. Taking care of big snakes is a huge responsibility. Is this the pet for you?

Read on and find out what makes boas and pythons such far-out and unusual pets.

This snake is getting ready to have dinner.

2

Wild About Snakes

What do you know about boas and pythons?
The one thing most people know is that they
can grow *really* big. But what would it be like to
own one? What kind of places do they live in? Do
they live in trees? Do they burrow underground?
The way boas and pythons live in the wild will give
you an idea of how they will behave as pets.

Boas like to hang out in trees. They can blend in with the tree to keep safe, and to surprise their prey.

Where Do Boas and Pythons Live?

Boas and pythons live in warm places. Boas can be found in parts of Central and South America. (Two kinds, the rosy boa and the rubber boa, can be found in western North America.) Boas can live in a variety of places, including deserts, grassy fields, woodlands, and rain forests. They may live in trees, on the ground, or burrow down below. The anaconda is the only kind of boa that lives in the water.

Pythons can be found in parts of Asia, India, the East Indies, Africa, Australia, and southern Mexico.

Most pythons live on the ground, but they are also good climbers and good swimmers.

The Big Squeeze

All snakes have sharp, needlelike teeth. But not all snakes are venomous. Venomous snakes have fangs that inject a poison (venom) into their prey.

Pythons and boas use their teeth to help catch and hold their prey before they squeeze it to death.

A green tree python is hatching from its egg.

This rubber boa baby was born live from its mother.

Far Out!

What's the Difference Between Boas and Pythons?

Boas and pythons have a number of differences. The biggest one is that boas give birth to live baby snakes and pythons lay eggs.

Prey may be a mouse or other small animal they hunt for food. But boas and pythons are not venomous snakes. They are constrictors. They squeeze their prey to death.

Constrictors grab and hold onto their prey with small, hooked teeth. Then they wrap their bodies

Boas and pythons don't chew their food—they just swallow it whole. This python is eating a bird.

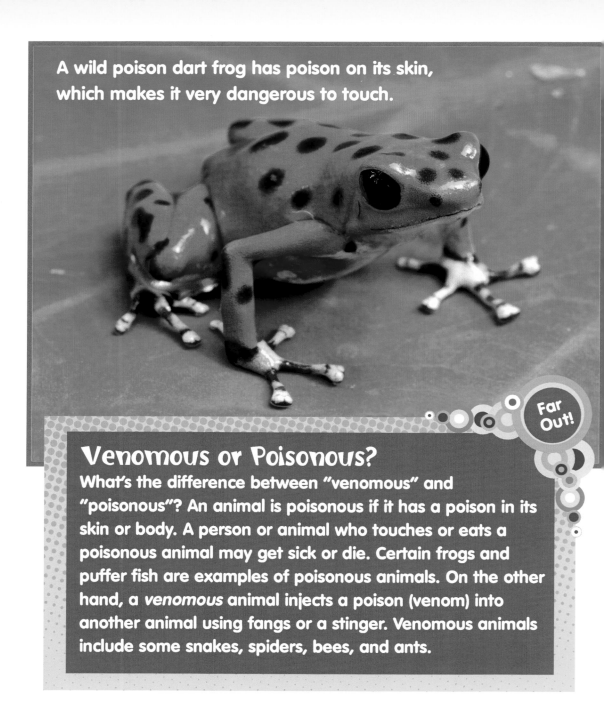

A wild poison dart frog has poison on its skin, which makes it very dangerous to touch.

Far Out!

Venomous or Poisonous?

What's the difference between "venomous" and "poisonous"? An animal is poisonous if it has a poison in its skin or body. A person or animal who touches or eats a poisonous animal may get sick or die. Certain frogs and puffer fish are examples of poisonous animals. On the other hand, a *venomous* animal injects a poison (venom) into another animal using fangs or a stinger. Venomous animals include some snakes, spiders, bees, and ants.

around the animal and squeeze tightly. This doesn't crush the animal's bones. The snake just holds its prey tightly. It keeps squeezing until the animal can no longer breathe.

Once the prey is dead, the snake loosens its grip and then swallows it whole! Snakes don't chew their food. The acid in their stomach is very strong. It can soften the animal's bones and skin and turn them into mush.

What kind of animals do these big snakes eat? Usually they are small animals such as fish, frogs, mice, birds, or lizards. However, some really big snakes can eat much larger prey, such as a pig or goat!

A Snake's Senses

Have you ever seen a snake flick its tongue in and out of its mouth? The tongue is forked. It looks a little scary, like it could sting you. But it is actually completely harmless. Snakes use their tongue strictly for smell. The tongue picks up scents in

Open Up Wide!

Can you imagine trying to stuff a whole watermelon into your mouth? That would be impossible. Your jaws can only open so wide. But a snake can eat an animal much larger than its head. How is that possible? Well, snakes have amazing jaws. Their jaws are held together by tough bands of tissue that can stretch like rubber bands. So a snake can open its mouth *really* wide. As the animal travels inside the snake's body, muscles stretch to let it through. You might even see the shape of the animal as it moves through the snake's body.

the air. It then brings them inside the mouth to two tiny pouches called the Jacobson's organ. This organ is very sensitive to smells. That is how snakes can locate food, find a mate, or spot an enemy. Snakes do have nostrils, but they use them only for breathing, not smelling.

Snakes use their tongues to smell the air to find out what's going on around them.

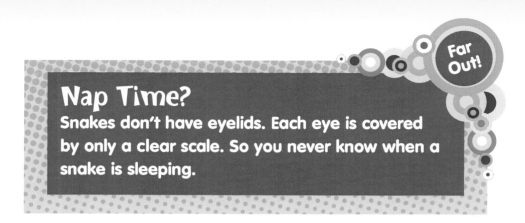

Nap Time?

Snakes don't have eyelids. Each eye is covered by only a clear scale. So you never know when a snake is sleeping.

Snakes do not have ears like we do. So they cannot hear sounds around them. However, they can feel sounds through vibrations. Vibrations are shaking movements. Snakes feel these movements in the ground through their jaw bones. They can feel a person's footsteps from many yards away. They can even feel a tiny mouse scurrying through the grass. The vibrations let the snake know how to react. The strong vibrations of a person's footsteps, for example, will likely scare the snake away. But the light vibrations made by the little mouse may draw the snake closer.

Besides vibrations, many boas and pythons have another way of finding prey. They can spot an

A boa's heat sensors are just above its upper lip.
They help the snake sense the heat of another animal.

animal by using special heat sensors. These are
found just above the upper lip. The heat sensors
can detect the body heat of warm-blooded animals,
such as mice and rats. The snake "sees" a glowing
"heat picture" of its prey.

3

You Want a Pet Python?

How cool would it be to own a boa or python? A newborn boa constrictor is about 18 inches (46 cm) long. It's so cute and easy to handle. The snake can easily wrap around your fingers. But it won't be this small for long. In just one year, it will grow to 3 feet (about 1 meter) long.

A baby boa constrictor can fit in your hand, but it may grow up to 10 feet long!

Eventually, it may grow as many as 7 or 8 feet (over 2 meters) more! Before you know it, you could have a 10-foot (3-meter) snake on your hands. Actually, you probably wouldn't even be able to hold a snake that big—at least not without help.

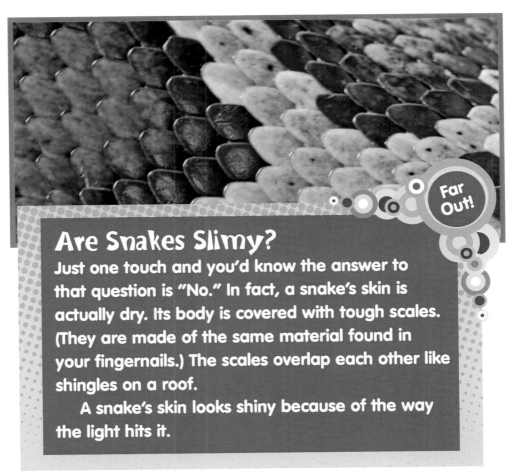

Far Out!

Are Snakes Slimy?

Just one touch and you'd know the answer to that question is "No." In fact, a snake's skin is actually dry. Its body is covered with tough scales. (They are made of the same material found in your fingernails.) The scales overlap each other like shingles on a roof.

A snake's skin looks shiny because of the way the light hits it.

Boas and pythons are cool no matter what their size. But a big one is a lot to handle. Let's take a closer look to see if this is the right pet for you.

A Close Look at Boas

There are over fifty different kinds of boas. Not all boas make good pets. Some are calmer than others. And some are larger than others.

Boas come in a variety of colors and markings. They may be tan, green, red, or yellow. Their markings may be jagged lines, ovals, diamond shapes, or circles.

Not all boas are giants. The average size is 5 to 10 feet (1.5 to 3 meters) long. But some may not grow more than 20 inches (50 cm) long. Others may reach as much as 13 feet (4 meters).

Common boa constrictors and red-tailed boas are popular pets. Common boas range from 6 to 9 feet (2 to 3 meters) long. Red-tailed constrictors are bigger than common boas. They may reach as much as 12 to 14 feet (3.7 to 4.3 meters) long,

Brazilian
rainbow
boa

Emerald tree boa

Brown boa

25

although the average length is 9 to 10 feet (2.7 to 3 meters). An adult boa can weigh more than 75 pounds (34 kg).

The rosy boa may be the ideal boa constrictor pet. It is small and calm. Rosy boas are much smaller than the average boa constrictors. They grow to only 2 to 3 feet (0.6 to 0.9 meter). In the wild, rosy boas are found in southern California, western and southern Arizona, and down into northwestern Mexico. These small boa pets are also easy to handle and can live for fifteen years or more.

This red-tailed boa is waiting for dinner to go by.

Rosy boas are a popular option if you want a pet boa.

A Close Look at Pythons

There are about fifty different kinds of pythons. In general, pythons tend to grow larger than boas. But like boas, not all pythons grow up to be giants.

Pythons grow to an average of 6 to 10 feet (1.8 to 3 meters) long. However, some may not reach more than 4 feet (1.2 meters) long. Others may grow to more than 20 feet (6 meters) and weigh over 200 pounds (91 kg)!

The ball python, originally from Africa, is probably the most popular python pet. It is smaller than the average python. It grows to about 4 to 6 feet (1.2 to 1.8 meters) long. If you see a ball python roll up into a tight ball, that means that it is stressed or scared. It tries to protect itself by hiding its head in the center of its curled-up body.

Ball pythons are very picky eaters and are known for going for long periods without food. Despite the feeding problem, they can live to twenty or more years.

33 feet

36 feet

Far Out!

World's Biggest Snakes

The longest snake on record was a reticulated python. It was 33 feet (close to 10 meters) long! But the heaviest snake was an anaconda. Its body was about 30 feet (9 meters) long and 3 feet (0.9 meter) wide. It weighed an estimated 500 pounds (227 kg)! It would take eight to ten strong men to lift this snake. Snakes that grow this big can eat an animal the size of a sheep, or even a person!

Where Do You Get Boa and Python Pets?

You don't want to snatch a snake from its home in the wild. You may not know what kind of snake it is. It may not be very friendly. Worse yet, it could be venomous.

The best place to buy a boa or python is from a responsible breeder. This is someone who specializes in raising these snakes. These breeders take good care of their snakes. They make sure

Ball pythons are popular pets for python fans.

Be sure to buy your pet python or boa from someone who really knows snakes.

they stay healthy. They handle their snakes often, as well. Breeders can give you information on the snakes' background. They can also answer any questions you might have.

An animal rescue shelter is another good place to look for boas and pythons. That's where a lot of unwanted constrictors end up. Many people don't realize what they're getting into when they buy these snakes. Once their cute little snakes grow several feet long, they find that they can no longer handle the responsibility.

Many pet stores sell boas and pythons. But this may not be the *best* choice. Unless the pet shop specializes in reptiles, workers often don't know a lot about the animals. They don't take care of the pets the way a breeder would. Pet store snakes are also more likely to have health problems. They may not be as tame and calm as those raised by a breeder, either.

An important question to ask a pet store or shelter is whether the snakes came from a breeder or were taken directly from the wild. Animals from a breeder are usually healthier and better eaters. In addition, taking snakes from the wild may cause problems in the wildlife populations. Mice and other animals they might have eaten may multiply and damage the plant life.

Pythons in Florida

Burmese pythons are taking over the Florida Everglades. Thousands of these snakes—many of which were once family pets—are becoming pests. They have been eating local wildlife and traveling into people's neighborhoods.

Burmese pythons are among the biggest of their kind, growing to more than 20 feet (6 meters) long. Their numbers have been growing fast since the 1990s. Pet owners often found that their snakes had grown too large to handle. So they took their python pets to the swamps and left them there.

It is never a good idea to release a boa or python pet in the wild. In cold places, the snakes could die. In warm places, such as Florida, the snakes can cause serious problems.

4

A Home for Your Snake

A boa or python is not the kind of pet you want to get loose in your house. You never know where the snake might show up. The snake may slide behind furniture or hide in closets. Or it may sneak up on you unexpectedly. Your mom or dad would not be too happy to find a huge snake getting cozy in their bed. Even worse, your pet could hurt someone. No matter how tame your snake seems to be, boas and pythons are still wild.

Boa and python pets must be kept in a large tank or cage. They do best when their tanks look and feel a lot like their homes in the wild.

Be sure to keep your pet boa or python in a cage to keep it safe.

All the Comforts of Home

A small boa or python can be kept in a 20-gallon aquarium tank. But larger snakes need more space—the bigger the better. You can keep an adult in a 30- to 50-gallon tank. The tank should be covered with a mesh lid to let air through.

Make sure the lid is clamped onto the tank *tightly*. Boas and pythons are expert escape artists. If there's a way to get out of their cage, they'll find it. These snakes are very strong. They will try to push out through the top if they can. You could put a pile of books on top of the tank and the snake would still try to lift the lid to make its escape.

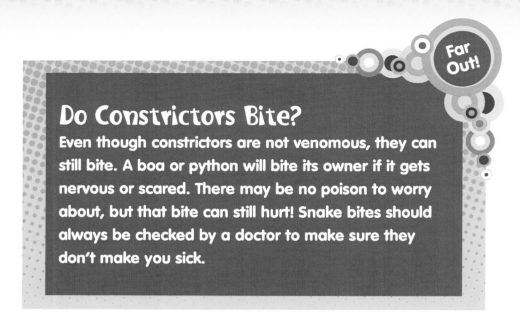

Do Constrictors Bite?

Even though constrictors are not venomous, they can still bite. A boa or python will bite its owner if it gets nervous or scared. There may be no poison to worry about, but that bite can still hurt! Snake bites should always be checked by a doctor to make sure they don't make you sick.

Pet suppliers also sell cages specially made for reptiles. For example, a large wire screen cage with a wood frame would be a good choice. It is more expensive than a tank. But it is easy to keep clean. It provides plenty of fresh air, as well. It is usually escape-proof, too. The cage should be at least 4 to 6 feet (1.2 to 1.8 meters) long to give the snake enough room to move around.

Cover the bottom of the tank or cage with a layer of bark or wood chips. Paper towels or newspapers work as well.

Snakes like to climb, so it is important to have heavy branches in their cage.

Cold-blooded animals, such as boas and pythons, need lots of warmth to stay healthy.

The snake's home should have rocks and thick, sturdy branches for climbing. It should also have hiding places, such as a turned-over, broken plant pot.

Heat is a very important part of a snake's home. Snakes are cold-blooded animals. That doesn't mean that their blood is always cold. It just means that their body temperature depends on the air around them. In cold places, they cool down. When it's hot, they heat up. Warm-blooded animals—such as cats, mice, and you—can warm or cool their own bodies to stay comfortable.

So your snake's home should be warm. If you place a heating pad under the cage, it will help keep the cage warm. During the day, the temperature should be 80°F to 85°F (27°C to 29°C). At night, the cage should be kept cooler. A temperature of around 75°F (23°C) will work best for your pet.

There should also be a basking spot. This is an area that is warmer than the rest of the cage. In the wild, snakes sometimes bask—lie in a sunny place, soaking up the heat. The sun's heat helps to warm up their bodies. You can use a heat lamp to make a basking spot in your snake's cage. The basking temperature should be about 90°F to 95°F (32°C to 35°C). Put a branch near the heat lamp so the snake can bask in the heat whenever it wants to.

Your snake should also have a water bowl. It should be large enough for the snake to lie in it and soak. Soaking in water will also help when the snake is shedding its skin.

My Snake Is Peeling!

From time to time, you may find pieces of skin peeling off your pet snake. Don't worry—it's not sick. As a snake grows, its tough, scaly skin may get too tight. New skin forms underneath, and the old skin peels off. A snake must shed its skin regularly as it grows. A healthy snake that has plenty of water usually sheds its whole skin in one piece. If you find a lot of small patches of shed skin, your snake probably needs more water.

This girl is holding her ball python in her arms.

It's Feeding Time!

Boas and pythons feed mainly on mice or small to medium-sized rats. You might have seen pictures of a big snake eating a live mouse or rat. But feeding your pet a live animal is not a good idea. The "prey" might fight back. If the snake isn't hungry, it may ignore it. Then the mouse or rat may bite and chew your pet. It could hurt your snake or possibly give it a disease. Snakes that eat live prey may get nasty. They are more likely to bite or attack.

Many pet owners buy frozen feeder mice or rats. This is much safer for the snake. (Be sure to thaw the food first!)

41

Helpful Hint

It's always a good idea to have a friend or family member with you when you feed or handle a pet boa or python.

Boas and pythons do not have to eat as often as other animals do. Young boas and pythons need to be fed every five to seven days. Older snakes can go longer without food. They should be fed once every two to four weeks. Bigger snakes need to eat larger rats or even rabbits.

Getting to Know Your Snake

Have you ever seen someone wrap a large boa constrictor around his or her neck? It might have been on TV or during an animal show. That boa was probably well trained by an expert. But you don't always know how a snake will behave. So it is very important to *never* wrap a constrictor around your neck.

If you want to train
your snake to be gentle,
it's best to start when it is
young. Handle it often
and very carefully.
Eventually, the snake will
learn to trust you. You
can allow your pet to
wrap around your fingers
or around your arm. But be careful not to let it
wrap around your waist. (You might not be able
to breathe.)

Boas and pythons should never be kept in
homes with babies and young children. It might
also be risky to keep them around other pets,
such as hamsters, guinea pigs, cats, and small
dogs. All of these can look like prey to a big snake.

Boas and pythons can dazzle you with their beautiful colors and unusual markings. It might be cool to wear your snake wrapped around your arm like a living bracelet. If you spend lots of time with your snake, it can become a part of your family. After all, these big guys can live a really long time—as many as twenty to thirty years!

Words to Know

acid—A sour-tasting substance that can break down some chemicals; very strong acids can burn holes in things.

bask—To lie in a warm spot.

breeder—Someone who cares for animals of a particular kind and raises their babies.

constrictor—A type of snake that kills animals by wrapping its long, thick body around them and squeezing them to death.

fangs—Long, pointed teeth that some animals have, such as snakes, dogs, and tigers.

heat sensor—A body structure that picks up heat energy, such as the body heat of an animal.

Jacobson's organ—A sense organ in some snakes, used to smell and taste.

prey—An animal that is hunted and eaten by other animals or people.

tissue—A body structure formed by cells of the same type that work together to do a particular job.

venom—Poison produced by animals such as snakes, insects, or spiders.

venomous—Referring to an animal that makes and uses a poison to defend itself through biting or stinging.

vibration (vye BRAY shun)—A shaking movement.

Learn More

Books

Aller, Ben, Mark K. Bayless, and Riley Campbell. *Red-Tailed Boas.* Neptune City, N.J.: T.F.H. Publications, Inc., 2006.

Bartlett, Patricia. *Pythons.* New York: Barrons, 2009.

Stone, Lynn M. *Boa Constrictors.* Vero Beach, Fla.: Rourke Pub., 2002.

Web Sites

National Geographic Kids: Boa Constrictor
<http://kids.nationalgeographic.com/kids/animals/creaturefeature/boa/>

San Diego Zoo: Reptiles: Boa
<http://www.sandiegozoo.org/animalbytes/t-boa.html>

Index